Two or more islands

Two or more islands

Diana Bridge

OTAGO

for Will,
Ben, Isabella, Francesca,
George, Cecilia
& Xanthe

Published by Otago University Press
Level 1, 398 Cumberland Street
Dunedin, New Zealand
university.press@otago.ac.nz
www.otago.ac.nz/press

First published 2019

ISBN 978-1-98-853162-5

Editor: Elizabeth Caffin
Design: Fiona Moffat
Front cover: Detail from Simon Kaan, *Untitled (Triptych) 11-15*, 2015, oil and ink on board and cedar, 1900 x 1900mm. Photography by Sam Hartnett, courtesy of the Sanderson Galley, Auckland. With the kind permission of Andrew Monteith and Galia Barhava-Monteith. Author photograph: Jonathan Hughes

Printed in China through Asia Pacific Offset

Contents

I

Re-visiting the magnolia

Last year it offered like a sacrament its complement
of cups. Now, chalices the colour of communion
wafers have loosened to let in the shocking red
of stamens, and boughs lack all rapport.

Is it the fault of the lime, through which I once
looked up as though through ribbed and shimmering glass?
The lime this year has lost its aptitude for synthesis.
Unspangled branches cross like tangled knitting.

My eye moves down. Since last I looked, each lower
branch has turned into a tray bearing its line of cups.
Standing upright at an independent angle, improbable
cadets in naval white, these are the latest offspring.

Obsessed with origin, we rake through records
and write memoir. So, go for descent. Forget epiphany.
Decipher knots and read striations in the jigsaw
of the bark like entries in an old tree's family history.

A Good Friday mind

for Alex Calder

It arrives in the manner of the Baptist's head.
Black-bordered, its saturated contours wrapped
in print. Behind it, rainbow and shadow rainbow,
lie the arcs of your obsession: blood and
fishing. Hooked fish and daggered history
await some final union. Fate, or coincidence,
your words had prophesied as much.
They open to enfold it.

It is the necessary sacrifice, the big one,
swamping the scarlet tableau that is Easter.
You are not a humble man but here,
in an Italian square, you cruciform your hands
like mild Hopkins to receive the host,
the gold and vermilion victim, iron-rich.
No need to reel it in. To despatch it,
you have your butcher's knife, your leaping mind,

a deadly brand of male mimicry. You do captor
and killer, call up a crowd. You do the victim:
disgusting, corporeal. You open the breastbone,
the flies. We are shocked already and it's too late
for shame as weaselly remnants of the big man's
entourage shift facts like counters. Where
is credence? He hears they don't believe him,
Moro, master of persuasion.

He howls out loud in the voice you give him.
In the end he lays aside the abstracts
he has never lived by, preferring
the intimate detail. Elena Ferrante upgraded
then pared to the core. Descartes
might laugh at women's talk, and so might you.
It's all that's left. It, too, will go.
As he must, he lays aside his wife, his children.

Another woman helps him with his raiment.
Pray for me who once was Agamemnon,
no more now than Hopkins' buckled bird,
its gold-vermilion gashed again
and again
and again. Done. Done in.
Someone saying that was too damn easy,
a tawdry flash before the fade.

~

Isaac and Iphigenia, the girl on the slab,
and that one fucked and filleted, carved up
as an example (note – in every sizzling scene
the girl is nameless). Taken, the victim, though his reach
extend to the Duomo, the top of Cathedral Rock.

Gods fall – when you give your verdict,
be sure to bring in Götterdämmerung and
give it in spurts of fire as well as blood.

I close the pages on particular tragedy and
pronounce the necessary finding. You possessed it.
As boy passed into man, and man returned to boy,
all along you had it, the Good Friday mind.
Behind you lie the arcs of your obsession,
spent in a bloody twining. At a distance,
a broken curve, compliant as a consort, dimly
predicts the next bend in the road.

Note:
The poem is a response to Allen Curnow's sequence 'Moro assassinato'.
Curnow was in Italy from April to June 1978, the period in which Italian Prime Minister Aldo
Moro, kidnapped by the Red Brigades, was held captive in an unknown location in Rome and
finally assassinated 55 days after his abduction. Not long after this shocking event, Curnow
wrote to his son of the possibility of 'abstract[ing] it into a poem for my new sequence' (*Simply
by Sailing in a New Direction: A biography*, Terry Sturm, Auckland University Press, 2017,
p. 514). The 'Moro assassinato' poems completed *An Incorrigible Music*.

Cover reflections

for Michael Jackson

1

Your cover is the khaki-green of earth, a colour that
distils soils and hints at your vocation. It frames a landscape:
Pencarrow – bisected by a dark defining strip,
the land reclining on its hip, before narrowing to a tail.
Somewhere further off it will vanish, as you vanished, an otter,
into the sea. Clouds are streaked with guano, although the birds –
there must be birds – have been absorbed. The foreshore
is bleak, stripped of all but breeds of bush, which angle
themselves against the wind's unbroken onslaught.
But the sand catches fire, there is a light coming off
the sea and even the sky looks ready to ignite,
were it not for those earth-coloured bands
that marry with the scene, holding the present steady.

2

The question is not whether, but how it will come back,
the land, the winter afternoon. Will it return in its raw state,
as a plenitude of little bays, each joined to its horizon,
the primitive, the unconstructed moment? Or shrink,
the instant you start trying to recall, to a handful
of windswept crescents – each one of which tugs at you,
eyes, mind, heart, and demands of you language?
Remember how, expended, a shimmering spot will dwindle
like a star. Words that hatch in its place let in contrast,
other homes and habitations that wash alongside
in your bloodstream. Washing Pencarrow out?

Someone will ask. Shaped by encounters with elsewhere,
you possess answers. No one more attuned to catch
the twang of solitude adjusting to the ancient, variously
grounded, call of home. But let them turn your cover over.
You were born to that backdrop, to rock-littered bays
where tussock grass is blown towards the shore. There,

puffs of pale colour transcribe the wind's elation.
Ivory through yellow, they light this stretch of beach,
witness to a kind of rapture in this unpeopled landscape,
passed on to your daughter, resilient as a gene.

Note:
Michael Jackson, anthropologist and poet. The cover of his selected poems, *Walking to Pencarrow*, was painted by his daughter.

Among the stacks

for Joseph Poon

The air is exhausted. Not rich and rotten,
like the reek of gannets packed close before take-off,
its smell is stale in its own airless way. Books
herded floor-to-ceiling are able to swing outwards
and reveal the life you're after. Or close on it:
old China holding out against the West,
safe as a colony of birds on a vertiginous head.
Not to be walked in on; not to be prised
open. Those who would learn her secrets
must pass through her channels.

To thread her passages you must have tussled
with the various nature of partition.
The groupings of the great imperial collections
are unfamiliar; entries cut up into dynasty and reign
fall into their curious categories and grades.
You would like to skim this storehouse book by
string-bound book, prompted less by industry
than intuition. But you are on the track
of one blue volume, one among thousands
in the mighty paper silo marked 'belles-lettres'.

You are seeking a surviving line we call original.
There is a moment – there, among the stacks –
when you feel the air has sharpened.
Just around the corner, you scent a passage,
or a poem. Now you are hyped up like a sybil
seized with divine afflatus. Arousal and
possession exist in heady balance;
call it connection rising to the surface.

You have seen the different kinds of leaf,
how they will overlap and briefly blend but never fuse.
So phrases touch while sense remains resistant.
You rein arousal in. It isn't long before
you tell yourself a leaf is nothing like a character.
You watch a finely printed row of them ease
out of their squares as meaning starts its slow bleed
to your side. It may not get there.

                              Meaning
goes down before a whirlpool of contending
claims. Only some of it will settle into words,
but when it does, you'll see old China compacted
to a line, as a range of blue-green hills
compacts below a bank of cloud.

Page from an Asian diary

It was straight out of this year's Asian diary:
a wall of water still as morning air. It filled the page
with blue, verging on grey. Its monumental form,
held in as though in sheaves, was patterned with
an ancient sign for water. So contained, it hung there,
tranquil as a curtain. Its import lay unguessed at.
In the bottom left-hand corner – a handful of dry strokes,
stamped with a red that bore no hint of warning –
a figure brittle as a house of sticks pursued her life.
Had she looked up at this colossal tower,
she would have seen it freeze into a kabuki pose,
intent not yet unleashed. This was no image from
'A Tour of Waterfalls'. Unsourced and eerie –
a freak imagining – it hovered overhead as I lay
flat, pinned in a scene I shared ahead of time
with helpless unknown others. I knew
no way to seal within engraved or painted borders
its unshed power, to sideline or waylay it.

Five hours on, a water dragon reared up over East Japan
and crashed down on a strip of coastal land.
Its buildings, all the life they held, shattered like brittle clay before it.

Encountering *The Book of Change*

Reach for what's at hand. It is always what you want.
Aphorisms froth in the tea this morning.
Here is another, a poet's warning.
Seamus Heaney delivers it: beware late Auden,
let in the sparkling polyvalent water of the image,
let go of labouring after truth – as if it issued
from the mantic sections of *The Book of Change*.

I hardly know what's meant by image there. A little self-
sufficient stand of lines throws up some architecture
in the heavens, an archetypal element of earth:
mountain, or pit. I see, not pictures, but a clue to name;
a broken line will yield an aperture, and so bear out
the name ascribed it: 'cooking pot' or 'well'.
In general, image seems to mean what is not word.

Yet think how the earliest heat-scarred marks
scratched on the shoulder bones of oxen,
on turtle shells, were answers, and in the manner
of an answer would be read. Imagine
the diviner: grey-green as unearthed bronze,
blurred as the outline of some blistered glyph
which, when made out, would surely counsel war.

To unroll symbol and to weave connection,
the lines and trigrams, and the trigrams doubled,
must be yoked to words. Summon up the shadowy
Duke of Zhou working on his pronouncements,
one to a line. Much like a song sung just beyond
the outer reaches of my hearing are the 'Wings',
the commentaries and judgements, as captivating

as they are remote. If you proceed, they counsel,
you will 'tread on the tail of the tiger'. To step . . . unbitten?
The judgement says, 'There is no failure, but Bright Light

instead.' To amplify, unearth a story from the Annals,
or cull from an old poem an allusion buried thigh-
deep in its rhyme. I see it now as once they saw it.
To surprise the tiger is, in this case, the right course to take.

In this case …? You mean your case. Put aside your scruples;
it's time to master trepidation, to move
from behind whatever post it is that shields you.
You know that divination needs a supplicant. So far
I've been content with chance connection,
coincidence breathtaking as the advent after rain
this morning of a snapping turtle –

nothing but serendipity when contemplating fire-cracks
on the undershell of turtles. Keep away, it will be laying,
they advise; and I avoid it as I would a call to war.
But now the turtle's image crouches in my path. Monolithic
as a rock, it has become the whole of Chinese culture
dumped there, saying, chip away, why don't you?
You ought. You know you ought.

J.H. Prynne in China

1

To begin with, you were on your own. Down
the rabbit hole, ideas welling; the fun, the fear of that.
From one word to another, as the gifted child saw,
was rowing between islands. Two or more
islands were cranes, fishing companionably close.
No special pattern to cranes. But feed in, not setting
but space, as the Chinese know space, and one day
the islands rise in a spray of swallows, godwits headed
for the far rim of the earth. Readable after a fashion.

Then came the time when you opened an index and
found there were two. Manichaean, then, the Chinese word?
No, nothing like that, just two arms of the track
they employ for hunting it down. You land
on the radical first. Oblique as a held spear,
quivering in shafts of live fur or disclosing
the balance inherent in wood, etching a shoulder
of roof. Meaning and mimicry blent
in a shower of dots.
                    You cross to part two.
Strokes line up by number under each root.
Brief units of sense, of sound, incoherent on their own.
To break open before you rebuild –
does that ring a bell? Fifteen strokes and counting.
The fragment glitters into not-quite-meaning
before the left side reaches out a hand
and there's the sparkle of ignition. So, is this
where you got it, your passion for syntax undone?

2

Words start in an underworld, its byways ready to be mined.
Those at home in the dusty tunnels of old texts discover
webs of origin. Endlessly paraded, the sources:
historical and legendary, cautionary, inspiring.

It's how you draw them out. Allusion shines its light
from the side. Examples only seem to strengthen.
Driven to re-invent, the best push on the door.
Du Fu did it, drunk with indignation, mad
with a fire that undoes structure. Lines

splinter under their load. Never a time when words
don't fracture. They fissure on the rack of politics.
No such thing as tense. It's true. Only last century,
small red-guard words disrupting everything. Revolution
carried too far. (But do we want what followed? Across
our planet calculation yields a crooked history.)
Mao was surely and severely wrong, but nonetheless
knew this. From contradictions arise new patches
of map. Grasp and apply. You take him up.

And then it rains, blotting out hardly the sun; there was never
much brightness. What is left? Young untried outlines.
Remember, from one word to another is rowing between
islands. Neither word new, nor brave, but together –
I know how this sounds – a universe, then. You,
as always, on the brink. We give ourselves to contiguity.
And the payoff? In the humdrum branches, in lieu
of revelation, are lumps of catch-your-breath
crystal. No more handholds. Just let go.

The gathering brain
for Duncan Campbell

The stepped hill is cut into mist. Although you know
it is made up of houses, a silhouette as numinous as this
calls up the near-obliterations of the Southern Song,
especially when the mist is pearly and rolls, softly, across
the throat of one hill then another, filling the gullies,
thickening behind the roof of the neighbour's
house, which hangs in air, a triangle trailing
an oblong, edged in the sun's first light.

The dawn bird invokes the whole round disk.
A second follows, and they cross from roof to tree
and back, weaving a buoyant message. Its view
is distanced, its claim not overstated: we live in a suburb,
the second largest in the country, but it still holds
a range of living hills. Sometimes, like today,
the hills we speak of float up from a base of mist
as subtle as the haze of any Xia Gui painting.

The collector's gathering brain connects the scene
to a half-text he once discovered. He remembers how,
years on, he stumbled on a complementary fragment
and coaxed the two into the whole his mind believed in,
the ideal text, the 101st Song imprint, which he,
failed scholar that he remained, dirt poor and well
below the men ranked first in the pecking order
of his society, now possessed; and the delight

with which he stamped it with his colophon:
'Huang, self-styled Master, passionate about Song printings.'

Note:
The Suzhou bibliophile Huang Pilie (1765–1825) famously possessed 'A Hundred Song
Imprints in a Single Shed'.

On Tinakori Hill

Pine needles are a sponge soaking up
the sound of our footsteps. Washed leaves
shine in the afterdrip of rain. The track winds up.
As the old song says, the way is dark and long;
the test is the path. Quarrelsome branches
scratch at us, neck to ankle, the small grudges
of the times. Far overhead, pines creak.
Pines tell of constancy. *The flowers*
will return in spring. Will you, my lord, be here?
Others, who do not know this,
will upend them. Life with its roots
in the air, and what grows
back, asking for help –
bulldozed.

That of course was later. The fifties
were an idyll, their catchword was preserve.
The women pressed down expertly
and hard on the lids of tall glass jars.
The children's eyes were on the fruit,
the luscious bottled globes of orange-gold.
One girl watched the water
as it poured over the edge, a perilous,
transparent, scalding spill.

She couldn't tell you
why, but she relished its escape.

'Morning Sun'

after Hopper

I have never seen a woman and a rectangle belong so well
together, she and it conjoined for all duration. In a slip
as pink as the Madonna's, she sits taking up the foreground.
The great square of the window tilts towards revelation –
there are the benchmark colours of the quattrocento,
terracotta backed by the blue of sky. Before it
she is as still and meditative as a saint.

                          Geometry,
insistent everywhere, re-routes us. Overlay, it says,
that medieval scene. The sun of 1952 lights up,
like funnels on a train, a line of chimneys
which cap a factory or a warehouse. The building
hurtles past. Slim blocks of pale green and black,
completed by an optimistic yellow, become
a theatre curtain, concertina-d to usher in
a sunlit, bold, industrial, new future.

                          And the woman,
does she embrace it? Sealed inside a vision so watertight
that it could pass for resolution, the woman keeps
her counsel. The great square of the window
tilts towards revelation. Only her mouth,
the brief willed gash of her mouth, denies it.

In the Garden of Flowing Fragrance

(Huntington Library, San Marino)

1

The garden is a spread of glinting summer greens,
multiplying as I note them, shifting sideways, upwards,
like a gathering of insects. It's not the wind –
it is my eye that's doing cartwheels. To try and steady it,
I lift from a sister art its way of observation.
Now the garden has turned hand scroll,
unfolding in a set of scenes that point up prospect
and find room for those small, charmingly
named, structures – belvederes and terraces,
pavilions and gazebos, which draw you in
for the prime purpose of having you look out.
Each leafy scene is mirrored in that complementary
element, the water, the green, unrippled
not quite passively reflecting lake.

2

'A garden leads to cultivation of the self' –
like the roof that wutong leaves have stitched above us,
the overarching credo. It, or something like it,
filtered through philosophies and poems,
is compressed into a bunch of couplets
to be read beside each entrance hall or gate.
For with the garden comes a package, which the place
draws gracefully, a train, behind. It is an export,
one of a family and founded on a template.
Around its neck is set the label 'timeless'.

But see how the skitter of Californian soil,
the streaming light-blue banner of the sky, define
the way a new-world earth receives the impress 'classic'.
In the air is transformation. The red of a small maple
that flares among cones of bonsai is singular and unpredicted.
As for those well-ordered sayings that travel single-file

down the sides of doors, each character, as though it were
an insect, must be trapped and re-examined here.

3

I hang over a bridge to watch brocaded carp
sport with another import, the sturdy Cantonese
who masterminds their feeding. Below, the fish,
broad-headed and importunate, turn into
a jostling gold and orange torrent. Fervently,
like a belief, this garden celebrates the present,
the gorgeous multifarious moment. Yet
every element is porous to an older balance.
Each branch and bud, as though it held a hotline
to the *Yijing*, most mysterious of the classics, discloses,
in numinous revelation of that old book's burden,
the one unwavering constant that is change.

Notes:
The wutong tree (*Firmiana simplex*), known as the Chinese parasol tree, has very large,
broad leaves.
Yijing (or *I-Ching*) is *The Book of Change*, also known as *The Book* (or *Classic*) *of Changes*.

Missing only the birds

Doors seal in the heat of another time. Warmth
seeps into joints braced against winter.
Inside the glasshouse orchids, drenched in colour
or white as a spray of Filipina brides, sway
in the wind from the punkah. Chains of coral,
lit sticks of incense, overflow their baskets;
tankas of crinkled seaweed float between temple
columns. Green everywhere is veined and welted
with its passionate opposite. A frangipani flower,
perfect as a new bride, has fallen on the stone path.
I think of a scent shed under dark branches,
of gardens thick with the temptations
of the jungle. Plants bank up like memories;
my cells open fast as tropical flowers.

Light came from the other side

1

I stood to one side in a field, waiting.
At my back, the spreading warmth of brick.
Light came from the other side, striking first
the feet. It grew, it travelled over the gentle
landscape of the stomach. The lower arms
had broken away, taking their objects with them.
Lotus and book remained; the conch, 'endless
spiral of the breath of Vishnu', was gone, though
my mind flooded with the shimmering attribution.
Word came from the guidebook; I straightened
before prophecy. At half past five precisely shafts
of sunlight struck the face. The god's expression
deepened. I saw the one that they name 'four-armed'
incarnate in the natural miracle of sunset.

2

Having stepped aside from metaphor and sacked
authority in one tradition, why re-install them
in a little Hindu temple in a field? You tread
a tourist track; you know that anywhere the questions
are the same. If you're looking for an answer, stay
with the Chandela sculptor, who drew upon the stunts
of the setting sun. Don't wrest your mind into deeper
murkier channels. Leave revelation at the god's look
burnished to surpass the standard sculpted smile.
And leave it there in its own landscape
with other restive atavistic longings. Leave
perception in its shell of wonder, as you watch
the sun go down on a tableau that will not be
translated into what it is you think you might have lost.

Note:
The Chandela dynasty ruled part of central India from the ninth to the thirteenth centuries.
The temple in which the statue of Vishnu chaturbhuja, four-armed Vishnu, stands belongs to
the southern group of temples at Kajuraho.

Going through Immigration

It was not as if I wore a sari.
I would have worn a sari, had I felt

entitled. I would have worn a sari
as I went through Immigration.

When I came back, and went through
Immigration, I wore a sari in my mind.

Zen

1

He named his boy Zen. No call
then for icons. A frog slips off his rock
into a pool stippled with rain. Spring
slippery with birth – or rebirth;
this is the monk's sly reminder.
Haiku, its lines taut, anchored, stretch
in a moment to trigger a flash flood
of revelation. Here is the world's
indelible landscape giving off
a truth that stuns.

2

birds
crossing the face of the hill,
the line of their flight
like notes of a flute –
requiem for those caught
in the dark of our unstable earth

You welcome that dry descant,
any image of air; welcome
even the unshackled rock,
now that you have gone down
to a place where images attenuate
and words will not take
the strain. Is there nothing
will release you?

3

Keep your mind on the mantra
and the I out of it, says the monk.

One day, not soon, the promised shift of gear.
What happened, happens and will happen

collapsed into a plane.
Attachment gone – the cleanness
of the separation.

No need to put it in another language
Sanskrit   Japanese
just say it as you once did
when you named him
in your own.

Was there ever an Avernus?

Hong Kong has swapped its daytime gloss for squares of neon.
Its showrooms are aflame. Lingerers propped in doorways
eye the crowds as they pour down the levels and the lanes of Central.
They watch as tourists watch, not in the way that I watch out
for you. All the way through you have brought up the rear,
the gap between us growing as we hit the crowded
channels of the MTR. When a train snakes into sight
a woman swims, a plump amphibian, between us,
severing you from us, cutting our trio clean in two. Doors
close; their rubber edges lock, an action irreversible as death.

Before it, our mouths open. Barbara's mimes 'North Point',
the name of the next junction. The two of us get out. Your carriage
rushes past, you hanging to a strap. We know you by
the bold banana-yellow of your borrowed coat. Signalling,
I run beside. It picks up speed. I run until I am slap up
against the entrance to a tunnel. You are headed for Hades,
a Wing On bag over one arm. For you, no boatman;
an infinitude of souls of whom you cannot ask
the way. No phone; not much Chinese; an address
that stops short at Qingshui wan.
                                    He'll work this out,
she offers, making for the platform of the returning train.
Around us, every way we look, wave upon wave
of others, each one dreaming of their home,
a square in some implausibly tall block.
We wait out nine more trains before we pack it in.
You are doomed to play the snakes and ladders
of the underground.
                      We make our own way down.
I think of Heaney and his bus. Aeneas, and the dead,
go down; the bus, a form of transport you can trust,
stays above ground. Rocked in our carriage, we sit grimly,
eating mints. In the face of separation no great poet
offers hope, just detail, lovingly inscribed, some hard to bear

allusion. And then, improbably, as if Eurydice herself
had made it back, a text announcing your return
arrives. Like Dante, I alight on the word mystery.

~

That night the moon rides high over the bay.
Unthreatened by our brief uncoupling, you sail into sleep.
In the morning you will tell me you were Theseus
in the maze, and had no earthly need of Ariadne;
and say – the trick is to add elbow-room with more
than one allusion – that you outwitted all your guides,
including Virgil. So, was there ever an Avernus?
A play of absence flickers through this scene. Seamus
has joined his friends, the classical dead, having gifted us
his own Book VI, a second version. Perhaps to say
that nothing has been lost. Perhaps to stay the pain of parting.
As before, some lines reflect a lasting separation.
And some, like moments in a game of hide and seek,
hold out heart-stopping promises of re-appearance.

Notes:
Qingshui wan: Clear Water Bay
Seamus Heaney's final collection, *Human Chain*, contains a twelve-part sequence, 'Route 110',
in which he 'plotted incidents from [his] own life against certain well-known episodes in
Book VI' of Virgil's *Aeneid*. Heaney completed his translation of the *Aeneid* in 2013, the year
of his death.

II

i In the corridors of old account

Callisto

To find design in the brute course of legend, bring on Ovid.
No matter that time and again it is, with him, the same theme.
Envisage, first, a skin made of cream, pink and patches
of primrose, Titian's living blend. Destined to darken
until it reaches chocolate, a shade ideal for the shaggy pelt,
the clot of paws. Transformation does not stop there.
Fur will stiffen into the dry mineral of stars.
Breathing form shrivelled into spaced and shining points
strewn, but not at random, across the sky –
now capable of being read: forwards, backwards.
We can, indeed we must be constantly decoding.
Ovid insists: join the dots and you will light
on Ursa Major and – what's here? – a smaller version.
Her divine rapist heard Callisto's cries and tossed
their son after her. Intending to assuage the chill,
the heat, the everlasting isolation of the stars.

Spare me another of Ovid's takes

A waxeye dives down
straight from the Garden of Eden
which speaks only of fall.

It's a tip-off.
Something lives
in the runnelled bark.
Rooted in the rough patch
of a neighbour's garden,
barely made out – I should let it be.
All I can really see is
the fluent life of the present.
Oh, spare me another of Ovid's takes.
But, before I can stop it,
the tree has turned into
one of his hybrids.
Now she rocks, quivers,
pleads like an obdurate tune.
Unwitting, like all of his heroes,
I've crossed some border.
Neither of us can break free.

Apollo holds all of the cards

From my window I make out Daphne,
so close she must always have been there –
there, among the catnip. Poor forked girl,
all minimal buttocks and striated thighs.
He is behind her, leaner, rampant –
one arm held longingly out. A topping
of hair that flops over his profile seems
to speak of a god's tendresse. He was shot
through the heart, told day and night
not to, but she, with her arms up-
flung, head turned, face hidden,
is the one who will incite pity.

Still here she is anchored. Identity
turned to wood. Her girl's life
finished; no dreams of untellable
tenderness. Her moment is fading,
now just a trick of the sun on
bark. No taste for oblivion either?
When art picks up the lines of the plot
her arboreal state must decide what
it can contrive. She who gave him
the slip will garland Apollo's winners.
A chorus of laurel leaves whispers
assent. Daphne will settle for salvage.

Add a name like Sappho

Add a name like Sappho
to your line and
you add more than you think.

As she steps, re-imagined,
out of legend, a cluster of compulsions
sounds to the strains of the lyre.

Here is classical aporia, grafted
onto creeds with newer-sounding names –
the springboard for all time remains

her legendary allure.

Note:
aporia, from ancient Greek, the idea of a productive absence, gap or obstacle, alluding to the
fragmentary nature of the few texts attributed to Sappho that are still extant.

In the corridors of old account

Antigone disdains degree.
When she campaigns for right
she shuns solutions brewed
in the convention centres
where her uncle feels at home.
Her sister's human hesitation
she eschews.

She stands, we're told,
for truth. Like any truth, her truth
is garmented in the half-truth
of particulars. Yet her name flames
in the corridors of old account.

No one can guess an ending

i: Penelope by night

You came in leopard skin,
warm-blooded to your feet. You came in black.
You came in siren colours and a short skirt.
Circe   Calypso   Nausicaa,
you offered talismans and toys,
threw in yourself. You stayed till
midnight and the whole ward
knew you weren't just any
island opening its shores,
but his Penelope.

ii: Companion piece

He navigates a rocky course.
Dead-ends and decoys dreamed up
by an adversary as able to change
strategies as shape. The drug
is poised like the four-handed god
between creation and destruction.
A stand-in for his fabled cunning.
See how I'm piling myth on myth. Long
odds is what I mean. Long odds
but he makes it. He makes it home.

iii: Interlude in an olive grove

He has gone outside to move among his olive trees,
which radiate in rows whichever way you look.

Each one matched to a name. To be joined
to a tree is a promise of perpetuation.

His scheme is simple. Parents, heart of the tribe,
set closest to the house. Alongside and behind,

the family. Friends, near and further out.
Two hundred trees are planned to celebrate

his loves and his connections. He mows the grass
around them, stopping at times to rest.

iv: No one can guess an ending

The mist floats in like smoke over his uncompleted
garden. From my perch

on the rugged coast, I sense the seaborne swish
of myth undoing myth.

At times a myth will open to align a life with legend
but no one can guess an ending.

And so she weaves from their lives' shape a finish.
Penelope completes the garden.

This is Demeter

Find her a mask. She can't speak without it, let alone sing.
Have her peer through mystery eyeholes, press her face
to the stiffness of wood, stand in close to the pitted stone
and inhale its buried smell, as though it went back
to the start; as though it were passed – a breath,
an imprint – figure through figure, unsettling shape
as it goes, all the way back to those grooves cut –
in grief or rapture – on the ochre sides of a block.

Here on the ground floor, she has come to what she knows,
this one, rooted in story. This is Demeter mourning
her daughter. She looks out on an earth that is in retreat.
Not a leaf scuffs its barren floor. Her gaze is a tunnel
and no sound spills from her mouth. Her grief is immutable.
Hand my mother that mask. Let her sing, let her scratch
at lines to her god, to loss, her daughter. Have her
make them in stone so, together, their grief is immutable.

Note:
A version of this poem appeared as 'In the museum' in *In the Supplementary Garden*.

A passionate possession

for George

He is five and he knows style when he meets it. Style
is all about line. He is drawn to the flare of the metal sail,
the arc of the polished base – crescent and square,
the oldest of all designs. I recognise enchantment

but go further and weave, from momentary likeness,
a lateral kind of truth. I toss out spiking neurons and synapses –
words a brush with science has you call on –
in favour of a salty, dark, free-flowing liquid.   I lie

but it's not Plato's sort of lie when I swap a language
of ignition for seaways in the brain; and say
he will as surely as Odysseus, in a ship we don't yet know
the name of, set out in his own flying crescent

on some god-haunted venture, leaving behind his women,
wife and mother; and return tempered, as turbulent men do.
If I let watery imagery prevail, here's the trigger –
the child's forehead billows like a sail.

ii *Out of chronicle*

The Henrys

1

How do you stand it, that spree of late medieval murder?

Head on, he says calmly, as if plucking a head from its basket.
Throwing scraps of belief at a coconut shy,
he is facing down horror.

His words scorch the freezing morning air.
While someone less vocal is sluicing the blood from the block,
he swings his lens wider; stops at the site

of a battle – rebellions are not hard to come by –
scanning the slaughter for some sign of good.
As if hope lay in the exchange of reigns!

Solace lies solely in the turning of the seasons,
the reappearance of flowers.

2

It's her turn now. Taking my elbow, making me look.

How does she face them, those Tudor murders,
most of them sanctioned? It's our history; we face it.

Script for a Tourneur or Webster, upping the carnage,
the rhetoric mounting as another one – priest,
wife or traitor – trails up the steps to the block.

For motive, she points out the cherubs in tapestry hangings.
Does she look to the past to cudgel the present?

Meanwhile, at evensong, mouths flare like trumpets
shouting the glory of king, of God.

Shakespeare in the Dell

These are the Players.
Tremble at what they bring.
As they strike their summer poses
and parade invincibility
they hint in silken imagery
at fatal symmetry within
each ancient tapestry. Time
to bring in the hero's destiny
and cloak in a fall of tears
the Fall of Troy.

These are the Players.
Tremble at what they bring.
What havoc have they
triggered as they fold
their garments, neatly box
their props, put crowns
and swords away?

Out of chronicle

Romeo steps out of chronicle.
Think of a deer caught in a thicket.

The dark that ushered in desire prompts
in this horrifying space no petulant hot licence,
the respond and lunge of earlier act,

just action cooled and turned against itself.
And choice at once so grim, so blind,
so true it brings us to our knees.

No one of us

The Players' play
is casting its beam on life.
Here it comes, flooding your stage,
your time too, with the comic-
photographic, the horrific-
tragic-pornographic.

No one of us today
is of the House of Corinth,
Denmark, Capulet –

Open your papers
on the boxed-up antics
of unzipped celebrity.
Read the cartoons. Turn
now to the latest unearthed
horror, the raft of killings,
in the bleak small towns –

Skip the exceptionalism
and forget those hoons.
No one of us today
is of the House of Atreus –

Just meet the Family,
I say.

Love?

Is it love comes into play
when, gently enough,
he lifts his daughter's braid
from her bent nape –

love that had her plait
her heavy uncut hair
ahead of time –

father and daughter both
concerned to ease
the passage of his sword?

Note:
During the Partition of India in 1947 many Sikh girls were killed by their fathers in order to
avoid their feared abduction and rape by men from other communities.

The end of the Raj

Last night they played the end of the Raj.
We learned that everyone involved was brave,
regretful and committed to solution,
each to his own; the English, late-
in-the-day, resourceful if constrained;
all of them powerless to contain
history's worst imagining,
the way it is with brothers,
the way it always is
with brothers.

They fight to the end, as they did
in the Mahabharat, that god-directed
slaughter. On these dark tracks
you may uncover burnished motives.
God does not make it better.
He may make it worse. Remember
he said nothing to warn Abel.
But you needn't look for motive.
It is enough these men
are brothers. Last night
they played the end
of the Raj. Again.

Note:
The Mahabharata is one of the two major Hindu epics. In a monumental narrative rich in
philosophical content, it depicts a war of succession between two groups of cousins, and the
devastating slaughter that ensues.

Brothers

Did a beer crate fall on those babies, breaking
the legs of just one? Does no one here know?
Both of them gone, both tiny boys,
one several days after the other.
They were *home*-killed?
Both of them?

If his smoke-scarred voice broke in half
at that point would you blame him?

As to the whānau, tight as Brethren,
you can't do a lot. They drink, they say,
to send those babies on their way.
Back to Rangi and Papa who,
everyone knows, should have
just hung onto them.

III

'Mine eyes dazzle'

Then I, my darling, for the first time in years,
took my eyes off your face and started seeing reasons.
First we adore and then we analyse, willing ourselves
to push aside the red-gold patterns of the surface
in search of underpinnings, the foundation, any base.

There is never a base. We end up with soil we'd be crazy
to think we can sift. We end up with dark broken
stuff we can't piece back together, dense now
with the murky networks of the earth.

Pierced ears

I hoped you would not pierce your perfect skin.
I thought you were too young to do it, to barter pain
for beauty. I spoke – too late – of mutilation.

It turned out that I loved the sight of them,
the hoops and drops, the shells and cupules hugging
your lobes with the aid of a slim gold pin;

and anyway the punctures were no more than that.
Now you have battle scars and wear them as a hero
under his breastplate. Powerless as Demeter

to protect, I watch you these days as you reach out
for your daughter, for whom you'd barter
anything in life. Your beauty, if you were asked.

A winter's tale

That is my title and, yes, it is a tale
that starts with rumour riffling summer leaves …

Of course she has done nothing wrong that flesh
so turn against her, and she require a Jobiad
of trials, each one entailing loss.

There is a point where plots diverge. I go
with mine, go with the words I've held at bay
all afternoon – now they slide into earshot.

A young breast is a thicket; it may need weeding.
Her breast is a thicket and needs weeding. This is poet's
language – persuasive as a violin, it would not

willingly mislead. Even so, I put aside my language
and learn theirs. The guardians of her breast,
like Shakespeare's own Paulina, are patient and ingenious.

They lift the tissue from its shell, scrape or suction,
I'm not sure, but when they've laid it all aside –
the perfect with the wayward cells – they resurrect.

Amazing what they do. Tissue you can inhabit,
a shape that is wholly your own. Think of a stitch taken up
to the seam, a palpable life woven right to the edge.

Then shining Hermione stepped from her case,
restored. And her daughter, straight as an arrow parting
the crowd, made it into her mother's arms.

This is where tales converge,
where life, placed on hold, resumes.

Dream analogue

I am set down in the lobby of the wrong hotel,
I cannot tell by whom. I know that just across the street,
a street I cannot seem to cross, is where I need to be.
No one here believes me. The mother is the one
who's meant to know the way. My daughter,
who is kind but busy, doesn't listen.

It is her daughter who holds onto me;
as we cross she clings like a koala to my back.
It doesn't matter where we go. You can be
lost and happy. In my dream I hope that all the lost
old souls of whom we read will find the way
to their known squares. And that they will be lighted.

Two poems for Francesca

1

My heart lifts when they come in the door.
It lifts when they go out, knowing they will be back.

I wave from the upstairs landing and life reverts
to normal. I pick up anything on offer, a book,

an article – whatever happens to be there.
No topic can eclipse her. No subject gifts itself

as she does when she simply lifts her face,
and I wonder where in the spectrum you would place

her eyes. Stored deep in their decided brown
are flashes of remembered life, trace elements of navy.

2

At bedtime we trade trust for trust. I stretch
for your moon, you for mine.

I enter your world's characters, its fountains
and its forests. I do not contain it.

You reach for your own store of words.
I hear them double. Something precise and princely

in the placing of your tongue alerts me. I am bent
on understanding, and will not mistake your 'candle'

for my 'thank you'. Years ago your mother taught me.
I watched her as she stopped and thought.

She thought for something like a minute before
she came up with her answer: 'orangey-red'.

When the time comes to hand you on, it must be
to those who listen, those who wait

for colour's soft conjunctions to turn up on your tongue.

They swing towards me

They swing towards me on the screen,
the way their brother did that time he powered
his trike downhill and his life floated, a balloon,

behind him. That day was her birthday – her 93rd.
She was proud like a Chinese to add an extra year.

I want them back, that three-year-old with bloodied knees,
two unscathed little girls, and my grandmother,
the hardest one of all now to recover.

Who is that small woman?

Who is that small woman with the wings of milk-white
hair sticking out from her skull like willpower?
In a gown taped shut as a shroud, clinging
tight to the bar of her frame, she veers
down a passage reserved for the soon-to-be-gone.
But – darling, I'm not dying yet.
Convict or imbecile, displaced child,
she careers all over the lino. Behind her
the hand of repeated review. She has cut
loose from an army of rules.
Risking her neck to make it in time,
she is on her way home.

Two views of the cherry tree in October

1

I see it first from a small window on the landing, a branch
that struggles to become a subject. Then my dry brush

is minting abstracts. And all the while that understated twig
can barely hold her, his ballerina blossom.

2

Close up, I am enveloped. Quick, throw yourself upon it,
as you used to. With luck you'll never reach past

the bunched thickness, that breast of blossom,
to feel the desiccated hardness at its back.

As we bore spring

We can bear endings
as we bore spring distributed
in circles on her coffin.

We can bear endings
like the rainbow's,
still within sight.

Peony 1

It stood, a ruffled trick in a crystal cone, on a plank
of glass. Its pink nudged the edge of white –

not quite the white of you in sumptuous silk
that afternoon although, like you, it was a wonder.

Peony 2

A peony comes up. It opens like the word
of God – you see it as if you were Paul.

It is sudden as love, it is once and for all.

~

Epiphany is for the young and ardent.
Those who are halfway through must just make do.

But to you who are more, much more, than halfway through,
unfurl your tired old wrists and twisted hands

and jump to the Gloria. In the end, epiphany will do.

Forget the Promised Land

Forget the Promised Land! What we are after
is one scene, no *one* scene – what we are
after is nothing less than the whole of childhood.

But is it their years or our own we plan to re-
possess when we start with a room
flung open to the harbour?

We are talking a time when there was less life
of the brain and more of the viscera.
We hanker – lord, how we hanker – after that time.

From the roof beams we have suspended swings
above a soft-landing of rugs that smother
and chafe the deep cork of the floor.

A pattern lies here: anything to protect as,
once, we were protected. And so it goes, our species.

Some lives

Some lives are finished down to the last square,
so finely balanced they could stop today.
Such lives might be stretched on the loom of symmetry.
Yours won't be one. Now, or later,
you're not about to say, my life has fallen into place.
You'd rather go flat out till Friday and, Friday having come,
keep at it through the weekend, ploughing on
with what you're doing, more or less on track,
supposing you're unlikely to be given time to finish

but, be that as it may, every so often will come a day
that has you firing on all cylinders, which is what you say
when last night's rainfall beads the inner seams of leaves
and makes of any flower able to hold rain a chalice;
when a triangle of sun in the courtyard reaches
the exact corner where you're sitting, at a table
pitted with your thoughts, and it strikes you
that it's not the 'how it all comes clear in the end'
that matters; it's to be in the thick of it, amongst friends,
yes that of course, but words, or figures even,
knowing that they have become as good as friends.

A pounamu paperweight

1

From the knotted driftwood of the carpet where it has fallen
it looks up, shiny as a grey-green frog half in,

half out of water. On the three-inch circle of its back,
like bruises healing, are streaks of yellowy agate. And it is true

that sometimes you can free a headache by pressing
to the places where it lurks the greenstone's solid cooling balm.

Wisps of charcoal, brush strokes in a landscape that will never
break the surface, are sorrow's sunken remnants.

2

In the distance, washed in silver, one of a band of children,
she plays on the flecked iridescent sand.

She is mature for six, and sensible, kind as a six-year-old
is kind, artistic in her way.

In the first months of her life she howled for hours on end,
as if for hurts just shown her, and in her eyes the bleak

blank trauma of existence. Oh, but she was honest with us.

The infant sadness she once harboured lies forgotten,
buried deep as veins in youthful arms.

And I no longer need, on her account, to probe dark seams
in the jade of talismans and charms.

IV
The Way a Stone Falls

I

how it begins

It banks the present as it happens, lets it settle,
then sifts it into a first draft. Memory procures it

for the record. Memory decides how it begins.

It begins with waiters: temple dancers that sway
along paved paths bearing small trays of offerings, hips

fluttering as they cross. Their voices are notes struck
from the gamelan. They belong with the strings

of magnolia spilling over the lip of the roof. They belong
in the panels of Angkor Wat, Prambanan, Borobudur.

II

models

i

In the turquoise waters of the pool flowers spin like skiffs –
frangipani blossoms short-lived as court girls.

There are not words for them, those bas-relief girls
in towering headgear. Their poignantly side-facing feet.

Come, in the week of a great poet's death, you must try.
Star burst of jewels on a collar bone, a sash

that stands up on its own. A profusion of pendants
at hip, arm and ankle, as much as a body will bear.

Their faces are those you can see all around you.
Lips pout, figures narrow like vases.

Here, in this town, lie the models for more than 2000 apsaras.

ii

You are on the wrong track. It was laid down in texts,
the width of a hip, the slant of an eye. Relationship

followed prescription. Did they carry them with them,
those Indian traders, their sculptures along with their myths?

More often than not we're talking of stories, of epics exported –
taken by water, then trickled like corn into furrows.

Spilled across borders, stiffening the spine of a chieftain,
propelling him into a king. Into more.

From Surya, the sun, will come Suryavarman;
from the king of the gods will spring Indravarman.

Notes:
a great poet: Seamus Heaney
apsaras: celestial dancers

III

Angkor Wat

i

Light makes irregular landing on the temple's silhouette,
carving angles into the unbroken face,

conjuring from flights of shallow stairs grooves as deep
as benches, every one a mirage – there's nowhere here to sit.

Five single towers shift in and out of focus. At chosen times
they fuse into peaks of the one sacred mountain, Meru,

home to the gods. The ground is a spreading shadow.
Just a foot above it, a row of roundels is uncovered:

the temple's buttoned hem. My eye, cleverer than a camera,
flits like a fantail between the staggered outline

and close-ups of worked stone. Light is the binding agent.

ii

What can we glean from lines of inscription, clothed in the Sanskrit
that gods understand; from writing on door frames and steles,

from later Khmer dedications? The curvaceous carvings,
as fine as the verses, beguile and reveal, then frustrate –

all you're likely to find is a name with the dates of a reign.
For a sense of the King, see him borne in procession,

his glory compressed into art. Every material surface
is dotted with flowers, the decorative delicate symbols of rank.

Above and around him, as if he were set in a lake, float
the paddles of fans and broad bells of parasols.

Their handles are lotus stems, upright, diagonal, crossing
the scene like a loose-woven warp. Hardly different in kind

from the grids of thrown spears which, further along,
surround other heroes. As if pattern protects.

iii

I'm talking of corridors coated with friezes. The clean line of contest,
the tug-of-war balance, the tiers of streamlined existence –

these belong to the world of ur-legend. Move on in time
to the great fields of battle and you come upon ordered commotion.

Armies headed by epic protagonists, sculpted large like islands
in oceans, tussle human, and demon, antagonists.

Sandals slipping, shirts stuck to our backs, we keep pace
with the route march of soldiers. No swimming against that current;

no resisting the tide of their spears. If you pause
it's to see where an arrow lands; to further attend is distraction.

IV
searching for Sita

The wall's shiny twisting surface, as it slides away to the right,
heaves with incessant action, like the back of a half-submerged beast.

From the seething stone emerge monkeys; heroes follow and demon
opponents, limbs flung into radical poses – haunches spread, legs

grounded and bent. Each share of the action a dynamic balance
of forces. With depiction so crowded, the drama is present, intense.

Here a chariot wheel is a roundel of calm, for this is the battle of Lanka.
We have reached the high point of the most reprised tale of all,

the great, the beloved, Ramayana. Our eyes seek the leading roles:
Ram, Lakhsman, his brother, and Sita – not a sign of her here,

though her rescue has captured the plot. Hanuman, head of his monkeys.
And, known by the fan of his arms held up in a candelabra,

kidnapper Ravana, would-be ravisher, king of the kingdom of Lanka.

coda
If you want something closer to causes, emotions, or
the epic enacted in dance,

if you want Sita thrown on a screen – then go south.

Note:
The Ramayana is the older of the two great Indian epics. It tells the story of Rama, prince and
heir to the kingdom of Ayodhya. Sita, his wife, was abducted by Ravana, the demon ruler of Sri
Lanka. Hanuman, general to the monkey king, supported Rama in the rescue of Sita and the
defeat of Ravana.

V

Arjuna

i

Arjuna had almond eyes, a fine-drawn mouth and
that preposterous beak that all the wayang have,

making of them creatures from another world, ogres
or birds – until you see their shadows step

into the dance. Easier, as you try to follow
the twists and turns of epic, to skip from shadow

than from those brilliant reds and royal blues,
the glittering golds and greens.

ii

One of the puppets is unpainted. Picked out
in pinpricks on receptive skin.

When I touch the rawhide, which is streaked and flawed
as an original should be, I take possession

of the saddest and most catastrophic story ever told.
Half a million units of a currency I cannot fathom

stand between us, myself and Arjuna in meditation,
the puppet I should most like to have owned.

iii

As you pass to the knot at the heart of the epic,
when he shoulders the slaughter to come,

you need colour to drain and words to withdraw;
to lay hold of cause, and for cause to recede

so that all that is left is arriving with him at an action.
Then you know why he rides into battle,

not blindly but guided, accepting, bereft.

iv

After the performance, what remains
of duty and decision, of the heaviness of action?

What lingers is a shadow cast alongside those last dying
profiles on the gallery's unlittered wall.

Notes:
wayang: shadow puppet
Arjuna: In the Bhagavad Gita, one of the Mahabharata's best-known sections, the hero Arjuna
is exhorted by his protector, the god Krishna, to lead his brothers into battle against his cousins.
Faced with an impossible dilemma, he is persuaded by Krishna's final argument to fulfil his
dharma, or act on his duty as a warrior.

VI

the missing

i

The heads have gone, the heads of princesses, of kings
and ministers, the glorious heads of gods, some

still connected to their torsos. A number of the best of them
are housed in the Musée Guimet.

A pedestal from which the statue has been struck
stands as a monument to anonymity. But not to them,

the victims of construction. Prisoners of war,
contenders for the job and common felons, they were othered,

all of them. Turned into slaves without a second thought.
They cut, dragged and piled stones to make the steps,

the bevelled plinths and terraces of the king's temples.
They died on the job like flies, or any despised species.

Kicked aside when they fell, buried to avoid the stink
a left corpse will give off, theirs were the feet, the hands,

the shoulders, over a million of them, on which these temples rose.

ii

Go nowhere near! Tell me why I should look?
The answer you know by now almost by rote:
to make sure that no one – no malice-filled misfit or
bigoted thug – will again turn his eye on a variant group,
an indicative type, and pick from the mainstream a colour,
a spot or atypical stripe; that no out-of-hand orator
spouting his creed, having snared the soft-handed,
the disciplined few, the lucky, the simply hard-working,
the Jew, will once more dispossess entire peasant classes
before swelling the ranks with those who wear
glasses – no one escapes but, give him his due,
at this point he's nailed the deviant you.

iii

What art do you make from the skulls of the killed?
Do you sit them on boxes, pedestals, stands? Stud
one with diamonds? Place a few behind glass?
Or just heap them up, as they seem to have done,
in a harvest so artless it has to be skilled.

You can't get away – it's instinct in each word.
Take harvest, for one; it shifts you from plenty to surplus,
then on to excess. You may play with the referent,
juggle the term, but the way that we move
from dispose to expel brings us slap up against it.

The files and the photographs cannot be wrong.
They merely confirm what we guessed all along.
We came with abstractions and Latinate nouns
to cover the handful of facts that we know.
We leave with the vast arranged fields of bones.

They blur into monuments, art of a kind.
And like art they will not let us go.

iv

I heard it was the Vietnamese who did it. As they
heaped up the skulls and built them into pyramids,
did they, the ancient enemy, regard each bony helmet
as a lesson in mortality? Or was it a case,
with all these dead, of nothing but good?

Did they let in the singly dead and, once let in,
was there that pity tinctured with love,
which had you clothe a ghastly greying globe in motley,
which saw you lift from its dirt bed the pitted bone
and wrap it in the warm stuff of your memory?

They did not; they felt nothing like that.
It's one thing to soliloquise a single skull. But say,
my young, quick-thinking, quizzical prince –
what would you have made of piles of petrified terror?

v

Bayon, outer gallery. Round objects set at intervals
make up an upper border.

See what they hold aloft as trophy: a line of severed heads.

Note:
de mortuis nihil nisi bonum: of the dead, nothing but good

VII

a worked stone

i

Think of the way a stone falls. When contesters come,
as they still come, when the mountain fires,

as it still fires near Prambanan, stones are shaken
to the ground. I don't mean boulders wrenched

from land that even now lies latent.
A worked stone is a member of the chorus.

When it falls a blueprint must be found
so that it can be turned, a dice in the palm,

and fitted back among its fellows.
A worked stone lives in its first context.

Such stones are reinstated.

ii

Restoration here is subtle, hand in glove with
settings. None more symbiotic than Ta Prohm.

At work around the back are men the ASI has hired
to stand beside a crane, fine-tuning the descent

of a huge block of stone. Its surface whiter
than the rest, it looks as if it has been cut

by those who stand about in sweat-stained singlets
guiding it with shouts, until it drops

into the precise place assigned it.
And instantly assumes an old and worn appearance.

Note:
ASI stands for the Archaeological Survey of India, which contributes to the restoration and
preservation of temples at Angkor.

VIII

a passage to India

i

Before we went she said,

Of all the wonders of my journey, I liked that tree,
the great tree growing through the roof, the most.

I think she meant the way that tree and temple
merged, as though in marriage.

ii

What I remember is the menace,
the jittery foreboding connected to a secret

buried in the story, film and novel.
There was that scene where goddesses

were strewn about as if they were uprooted trees.
We are re-enacting how they came upon it,

the shock of finding a bare-breasted woman
lying on her side in the voluptuous jungle, bound

with creeper, the pillar of her thighs forced
open by insistent tendrils.

The way the greenery is left unchecked, the Indian way.

iii at Ta Prohm

Sunlight has opened door upon door of the god's house,
opened them upon a glut of statues.

Today it is a geisha house where strangler fig embraces
gateway. More slowly than an elephant

a courtyard kneels, its slide held up by ashen-coloured roots.
The scene is fin de siècle,

seeming to say there is more beauty in decadent conjunction
than regular performance. By that

I mean the upright functioning of mainstream practice,
nothing askew.

IX

step by step

i

Late afternoon and no one here at Banteay Samré,
the only intersection one of angles

as the long shaded strip of the causeway
meets with steps, and the steps with a cruciform terrace,

which looks out on laterite walls and an unfamiliar breed
of lion paired and planted each side of the stairs.

There's only one tower and a sense of elegant compactness.

This is building as secure as he who planned it,
the king's right hand, they say.

ii

We walk together up the outsize slabs. We walk
in the steps of kings, in pursuit of gods

that mean nothing to those we grew up with.
You read from the guide book, I look.

Together, we assemble from eroded surfaces –
side panels and the deep-relief of lintels –

a parade which once transfigured, for all we know
may still transfigure lives.

iii

And so to stairs. I go up stairs in the way she taught me,
slanted forward in a soft stretch: spine angled,

a rod over water, each haunch thrust back in turn,
clenching a strip of muscle from the sash that swathes

the hip, leg brought down like a lever, heel first.
This movement, in time, I bring to the high stairs

of temples, those stone blocks that rise, step
by step, to heaven, and the last view.

at Angkor, Yogyakarta & Borobudur

Acknowledgements

My thanks to the following journals, where a number of these poems first appeared: *Cyphers, Cordite Review, JAAM, Landfall, Meanjin, PN Review, Raritan* and *Warwick Review.*